Wind

DISCOVERING AIR IN MOTION

OLGA FADEEVA

TRANSLATED BY LENA TRAER

EERDMANS BOOKS FOR YOUNG READERS

GRAND RAPIDS, MICHIGAN

where does the wind come from?

Maybe there are giants,
hiding between the mountains,
who blow air
with all their might?

Or maybe it's the
trees swaying
that creates the wind?

Or does the wind come
from a windmill?
There must be a reason
they're called *wind*mills.

Or maybe the wind comes
from the wings of a large bird?

What do you think?

what is wind?

Wind is the horizontal movement of air over the surface of the Earth.

It happens because of differences in air pressure within our atmosphere,
caused by the uneven heating of the Earth by the Sun.
Air under high pressure moves toward areas of low pressure,
creating the horizontal flow of the wind.

what are the different types of wind?

Most areas of Earth have prevailing winds, which blow throughout the year from one direction to another. These vary by latitude (the distance, measured in degrees, north or south of Earth's equator). Most commonly, winds blow from the east near the poles and in the areas surrounding the equator, and from the west in the middle latitudes.

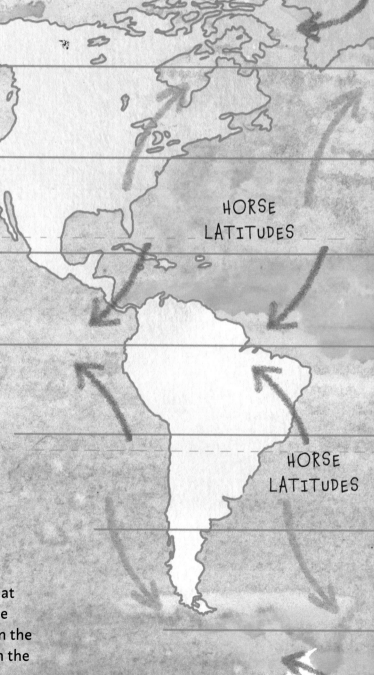

TRADE WINDS are prevailing winds that blow from the tropics toward the equator. These were sailors' favorite winds: the term originally derived from the early fourteenth-century sense of "trade," meaning "path" or "track." Trade winds blow from the northeast in the northern hemisphere and from the southeast in the southern hemisphere. They were used to ship spices, food, and goods.

PREVAILING WESTERLIES blow from the tropics toward the middle latitudes. They are strongest in the winter. These winds are mostly from the southwest in the northern hemisphere and from the northwest in the southern hemisphere. The latitudes where they develop are known as the Roaring Forties, Furious Fifties, and Shrieking Sixties. Landmasses slow down winds, so in the southern hemisphere—where there is less land—the westerlies are stronger and faster.

POLAR EASTERLIES are prevailing winds that blow from the north and south poles toward the middle latitudes. They are from the northeast in the northern hemisphere and from the southeast in the southern hemisphere.

HORSE LATITUDES

HORSE LATITUDES

HORSE LATITUDES are the windless areas in the Atlantic Ocean located between 30 and 35 degrees north and south of the equator. In the sixteenth and seventeenth centuries, ships transporting horses from Europe to the Americas often became stranded in mid-ocean in those latitudes. Water shortages forced the ships' crews to throw the animals overboard.

POLAR EASTERLIES

PREVAILING WESTERLIES

TRADE WINDS

TRADE WINDS

PREVAILING WESTERLIES

POLAR EASTERLIES

60°

40°

20°

Equator 0°

20°

40°

60°

Are there other types of wind?

In addition to the steady prevailing winds, there are also periodic winds: monsoons, land and sea breezes, and many other local winds. They all affect the daily weather and long-term climate in different regions.

PERIODIC WINDS are seasonal winds that change their direction every six months. Together with prevailing winds, periodic winds create a global system of air movement called atmospheric circulation.

MONSOONS are periodic winds that reverse their direction twice a year. They are most likely to form in the tropics, in places where a large continental landmass meets a major body of water. In the summer, the ocean air is cooler and denser, creating an area of high air pressure, while the air over the land is warmer, creating an area of low air pressure. The wind will blow from the ocean to the land and bring lots and lots of rain. When monsoons meet trade winds, they can cause rapidly rotating storms called tropical cyclones to form over Earth's oceans. Sometimes these cyclones can get big enough to be hurricanes.

In the mountains, even the smallest difference in elevation causes the wind to change speed.

LOCAL WINDS are winds that blow over a specific, limited area. They are influenced by local geography (including bodies of water and mountain ranges). Each local wind has its own name and character, such as the mistral (a wind that blows from southern France toward the Mediterranean Sea), the Loo (a hot summer wind that blows over the plains of India and Pakistan), and the simoom (a dusty wind that blows in the Sahara, the Middle East, and the deserts of the Arabian Peninsula).

BREEZES are one of the most familiar types of local winds. They form near large bodies of water due to differences in air and water temperatures and reverse their direction twice every twenty-four hours. Thanks to breezes, we can feel a refreshing coolness by the sea or a lake, even on a hot day.

LAND BREEZE

More often than not, local and weak, irregular winds die down at night. This is due to the fact that differences in air and water temperatures often become less pronounced at night.

SEA BREEZE

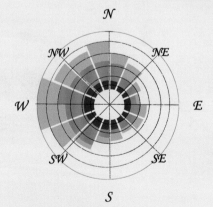

A WIND ROSE is used to display how wind speed and direction are typically distributed at a particular location.

How do we describe wind speed?

Wind speed is estimated using the Beaufort wind scale, created in 1805 by Sir Francis Beaufort, an admiral in the British navy. The scale goes from 0 to 12. Wind is measured in knots, or nautical miles per hour. One knot is equivalent to 1.15 miles per hour.

0

0–1 knots
(nautical miles
per hour)

CALM

1

1–3 knots

LIGHT
AIR

2

4–6 knots

LIGHT
BREEZE

3

7–10 knots

GENTLE
BREEZE

4

11–16 knots

MODERATE
BREEZE

5

17–21 knots

FRESH
BREEZE

6

22–27 knots

STRONG
BREEZE

7
28–33 knots
NEAR GALE

8
34–40 knots
GALE

9
41–47 knots
SEVERE GALE

The fastest wind speed ever recorded on Earth came from a gust during Tropical Cyclone Olivia that passed by Barrow Island, Australia, on April 10, 1996. It was 220 knots (253 mph).

ATTENTION! STORM WARNING!

ATTENTION! STORM WARNING!

48–55 knots   56–63 knots   64–71 knots

STORM   VIOLENT STORM   HURRICANE

What happens in a hurricane?

Hurricanes are often given names. This is done to avoid confusion when sharing important information in the news, weather reports, and storm warnings. For hurricanes in the Atlantic Ocean, there is a list of names that is used in rotation and recycled every six years. The first hurricane of any given year usually receives a name starting with an A. When a hurricane is exceptionally strong and catastrophic, like Hurricane Katrina in 2005, its name is retired and never used again.

Strong hurricanes most frequently form in the tropics. In Southeast Asia, they are called typhoons.

During a hurricane, it's important to follow guidance from emergency personnel. Unless there's a need to evacuate, it's generally safest to stay inside your home. If you are caught outside in a windstorm, keep away from sheds, power lines, billboards, and trees. Don't walk along the sides of buildings. Take cover inside a secure shelter as soon as possible.

The word "hurricane" was derived from "Hurakán," the name of the Mayan god of wind, storm, and fire.

THE HURRICANE PASSED THROUGH THE CITY, AND NO ONE WAS HURT.

How do sand grains travel?

DUNES are mounds of sand in a desert or along a beach. They resemble ocean waves, "frozen" in an instant of time, but contrary to their appearance, they are constantly on the move. Wind can change their shape, and they can move from several inches to over 300 feet a year, covering roads, fields, and trees with sand.

When a gust of wind carries many sand grains, the grains hit hard rocks at high speeds, gradually destroying, grinding, and smoothing them out. A masterful sculptor, wind can create fantastical landforms such as mushroom rocks. These rocks are worn away at the bottom because wind can only lift the sand up a few yards into the air. Mushroom rocks can be found in places like Goblin Valley State Park in the US, Sierra de Organos National Park in Mexico, Gülşehir, Turkey, and other places around the world.

With strong gusts of wind, sand grains from the Sahara Desert can cross the Atlantic Ocean and reach the North American coast.

How does the wind help plants and animals?

Without wind, many plants on Earth could not be pollinated. Pine trees and firs, willow and birch trees, grains and corn, nettles, palm trees, and many others are wind-pollinated plants. The flowers of such plants are typically dull in color, with little to no scent or nectar, because they do not need to attract bees. They instead produce large amounts of pollen, which is then carried on the wind. The pollen ideally lands on other plants of the same type, allowing them to reproduce.

Many plants rely on wind to carry their seeds. The seeds can travel long distances, tens of thousands of feet. Dandelion, thistle, and burdock seeds have a parachute structure. Maple, ash, and birch tree seeds have wings. And some plants—orchids, for example—have such tiny seeds that they can easily move through the air without any additional support. Eventually the seed lands on the ground, where—if conditions are right—it may grow into a new plant.

By carrying scents, the wind helps animals search for other animals, water, and food. It also helps them sense approaching danger.

which way does the wind blow?

When someone says a "southwest wind," that means that the wind is coming from the southwest.

A WEATHER VANE is an instrument used for showing the direction of the wind. One of the oldest weather vanes was located on top of the Tower of the Winds in Athens, Greece. The tower was built about 100–50 BC and also had a water clock and sundials, which were used to measure the flow of time. It is considered one of the first meteorological stations. The tower is decorated with depictions of eight wind gods. Its weather vane in the form of the sea god Triton did not survive to the present day.

A WIND SOCK is a simple contraption for measuring wind direction and speed, typically used at airports. Modern scientists also use a device called an ANEMOMETER to measure wind speed.

Belfry of Ghent
(Ghent, Belgium)

Tower of London
(London, UK)

Tower of the Winds
(Athens, Greece)

WIND SOCK

Admiralty Building
(Saint Petersburg,
Russia)

Town Hall Tower
(Tallinn, Estonia)

Riga cathedral
(Riga, Latvia)

Old North Church
(Boston, U.S.A.)

ANCIENT EGYPTIAN TRADING SHIP

ROMAN BATTLESHIP

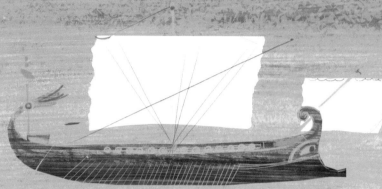

VIKING SHIP

RUSSIAN LODYA

How does wind help sailing ships travel?

Wind had utmost importance for seafaring. The first sailing boats appeared in ancient Egypt and Phoenicia in the third millennium BC. Before harnessing the power of the wind, vessels had been either propelled by rowing or pulled from shore by animals and humans.

The rise of trading goods and the desire to conquer new territories brought about the development of shipbuilding. At first, the vessels had one large, rectangular sail. This was difficult to control and only allowed the ship to sail when the wind was blowing from behind. With headwinds, the sail would be put away, and rowers would take over. Such ships were used by the ancient Phoenicians, Etruscans, Greeks, and Romans. The Vikings and the Slavs had similar boats.

The invention of a triangular sail—the lateen sail—revolutionized sea travel. It enabled the ship to tack into the wind, meaning that it could sail in almost any direction. How is that even possible, you ask?

MEDITERRANEAN SHIP
WITH A LATEEN SAIL

How can you sail into the wind?

Technically speaking, it's not possible to sail directly into the wind. However, if the wind blows against the boat at an angle, it can propel the vessel forward. This is called windward sailing.

As the wind pushes the triangular sail, water resistance prevents the boat from moving sideways, and the boat is propelled forward at an angle to the wind. So then, how do you stay on track? Having traveled this way for a bit, you'd need to change course and move in the other direction, staying at the same angle to the wind. The ship zigzags back and forth. In sailing terminology, this is called TACKING. How long to sail on one tack, and at what angle to the wind, are the important questions of sailing.

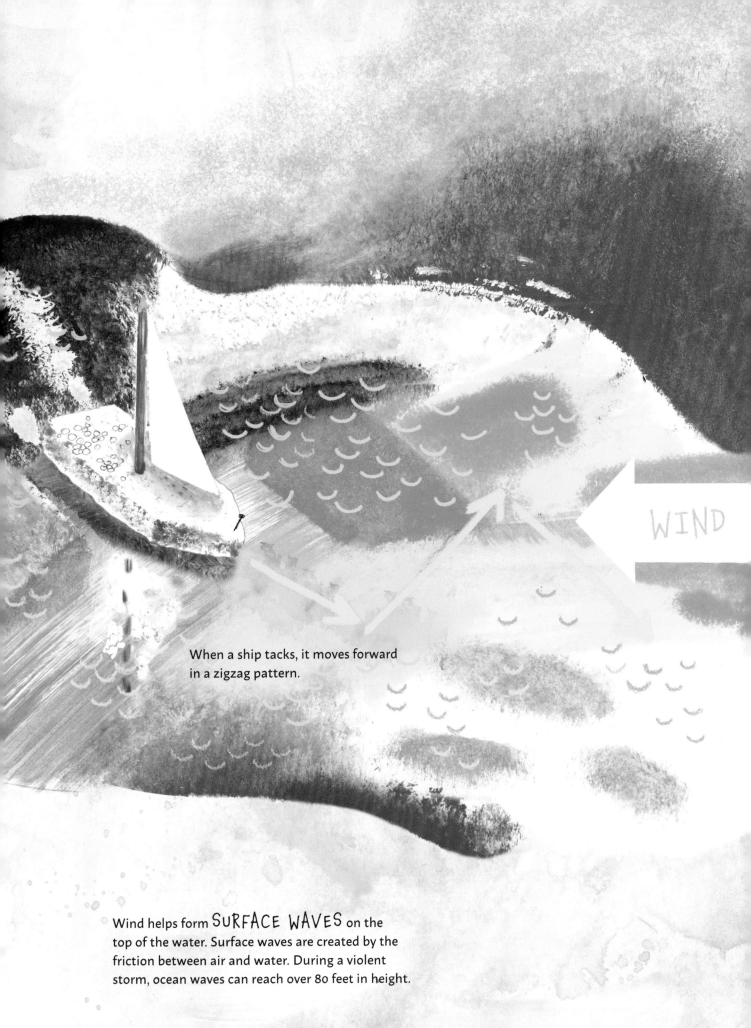

WIND

When a ship tacks, it moves forward in a zigzag pattern.

Wind helps form SURFACE WAVES on the top of the water. Surface waves are created by the friction between air and water. During a violent storm, ocean waves can reach over 80 feet in height.

At 60 to 100 feet above the ground, the wind blows faster than when it is close to Earth's surface. This is called the wind gradient.

This "carrack" design is a common design of ships used between the fourteenth and seventeenth centuries.

The ships used during the Age of Exploration could travel at speeds of 7.8 to 9.5 knots (9 to 11 mph).

The bigger the sail area of a ship, the more wind it can catch.

How has the wind affected history?

The fifteenth century saw the rise of the full-rigged ship, which had three masts and multiple sails. Traveling longer distances would have been impossible without such improvements. This marked the beginning of the Age of Exploration.

One of the fastest sailing ships in history was the tea clipper *Thermopylae*, built in the mid-nineteenth century. Why was it called a "tea clipper"? It was designed in the UK for the China tea trade. The ship had to move at an incredible speed so that the tea would not get damp or damaged in the cargo hold during the voyage. The *Thermopylae* set a speed record, sailing from Shanghai to London in 105 days. It had more than 36,000 square feet of sails—a total area of roughly half the size of a soccer field.

what about now?

Today, sailboats are rarely used for shipping and international travel. But many people still love to spend their days in sailboats on deep rivers, lakes, and oceans. Sailing is also an Olympic sport, with medals awarded for different types of races.

Many modern yachts have sails. By harnessing the power of the wind, you save fuel.

The *Hydroptère* is the fastest modern sailboat, capable of traveling at a speed of up to 52 knots (60 mph).

A windmill's blades rotate as they catch the wind.

Wind power is a sustainable and renewable source of energy.

What are other ways we harness wind power?

Even in ancient times, people understood that wind had enormous power, which humans could use to complete tasks. The earliest known windmills (used for grinding grain to make bread and other foods) date back over a thousand years to ancient Persia. In Europe, the first windmills appeared in the twelfth century. Later on, wind energy was used not only to grind grain but also to drain marshes, manufacture paper, and make vegetable oil.

The first wind power plant was built in Denmark at the end of the nineteenth century. Now wind power is the world's second-largest renewable energy source. Five countries—China, the United States, Germany, the UK, and India—generate over half of the world's wind electricity.

How else do we use wind?

It would be impossible to fly a kite without wind.

Kites first appeared in China in the second century BC. They were used for signaling and for scaring away enemy soldiers. But before the kite became something used just for fun, it played a role in scientific research.

Both American scientist Benjamin Franklin (1706–1790) and Russian scientist Mikhail Lomonosov (1711–1765) conducted important experiments with kites, which helped them make important discoveries about the nature of lightning and electricity in the atmosphere.

How does wind affect birds?

Wind direction and wind speed affect birds' flying speed and altitude, especially during seasonal migrations. When there are strong headwinds (wind moving in an opposing direction), birds will fly lower to the ground, where the wind is weaker. When there is a tailwind (wind moving in the same direction), birds will fly higher—and be able to move faster with the wind's help. Sometimes birds gather in large flocks and wait for a tailwind, so they can take one long-distance nonstop flight.

How does wind affect airplanes?

What if we go higher up, above the birds, to where the airplanes fly?
Does wind affect airplanes, too? Absolutely!

Wind direction and wind speed are important during takeoff and landing. Most modern aircraft do not take off or land with crosswind speeds higher than 33 knots (38 mph) and tailwind speeds higher than 9.5 knots (11 mph). Airplanes take off and land into the wind. Why? It may seem that it'd be easier to do this with a tailwind, but that's not the case. With tailwind, the speed of the aircraft increases: it moves too fast and may run out of runway. Runways are built to align with historical wind patterns specific to each airport. If you have ever flown in an airplane, you've likely noticed that flying in one direction always takes slightly longer. That, too, is because of global wind patterns.

Are there winds in outer space?

What if we go even higher up, above the airplanes? Or even higher than that?

What if we go into space? There is no wind in outer space, is there?

There are solar winds in outer space, though they're different than winds on Earth. Solar winds are streams of charged particles released from the upper part of the Sun's atmosphere. They don't blow horizontally, like the winds we know on Earth's surface.

In our solar system, many planets have strong winds, including Jupiter, Venus, and Saturn. Winds only exist on planets that have an atmosphere, like Earth. The strongest wind astronomers have measured so far is on Neptune. This planet is located far from the Sun but has an unknown source of internal energy. The amount of heat Neptune radiates into the surrounding cold space creates huge temperature differences. This causes windstorms. Winds on Neptune can reach up to 1166 knots (1342 mph). Such speeds are many times higher than the most powerful hurricanes on Earth.

IT APPEARS THERE WAS SOME OTHER TEXT

HERE,

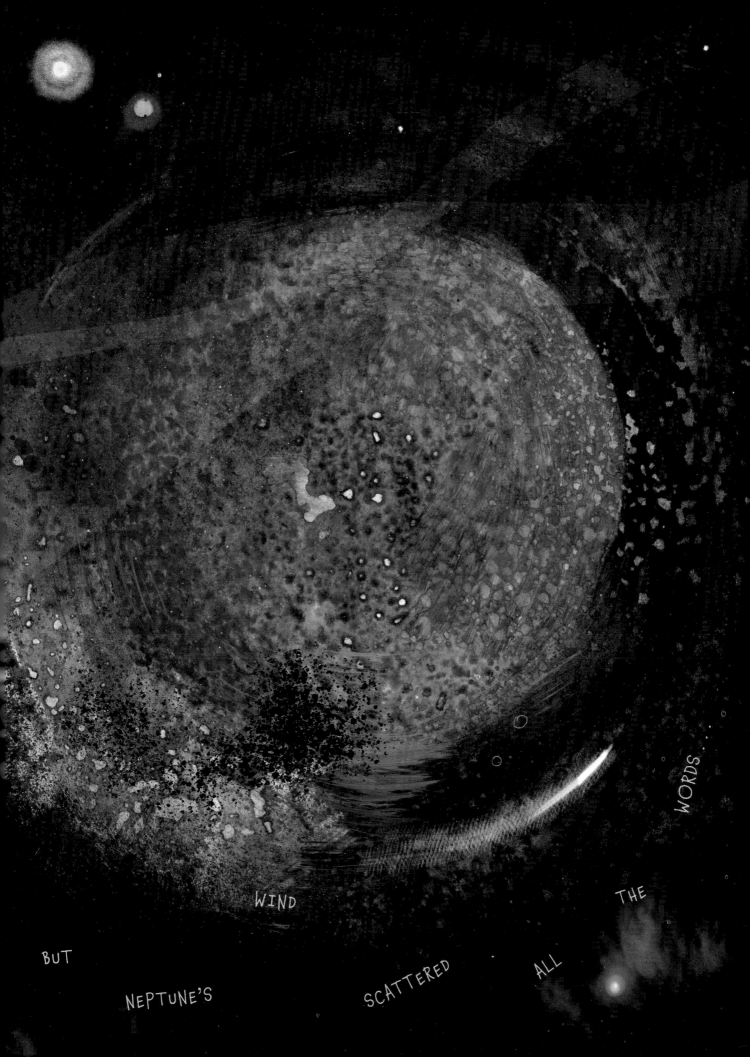

BUT NEPTUNE'S WIND SCATTERED ALL THE WORDS

~ A FEW OTHER WIND FACTS ~

Strong winds can make you feel colder. For example, 50 degrees Fahrenheit can feel like only 45 degrees if there's a wind of 13 knots (15 mph). This is called windchill.

HANDHELD WIND

Because of how important wind is to sailing, there have been many seafaring rituals to call the wind. Many sailors once thought that whistling would bring on stronger wind. Others would try to call up wind by throwing a mop overboard or scraping the mast on the side they wished the wind would come from.

Many sports could not exist without wind—such as windsurfing, kitesurfing, kitewing, wingsuit flying, and kite buggying.

Windsurfers can reach a speed of 54 knots (62 mph).

Wind has even changed the course of history. In the thirteenth century, the Mongolian invasion of Japan was stopped twice by typhoons, known in Japan as "kamikaze" or "diving wind." In the sixteenth century, another storm destroyed many of the ships of the "invincible" Spanish armada, which had set out to attack England—allowing the armada to be defeated.

In ancient times, wind gods were among the most worshipped deities. Here are a few of the wind gods that humans have recognized over the years:

AEOLUS — keeper of the wind in ancient Greece

STRIBOG — Slavic god of the wind

FEI LIAN — Chinese god of the wind

FUJIN — Japanese god of the wind

AMUN — god of the wind in ancient Egypt

NJORD — Norse god of the wind

WELLINGTON, NEW ZEALAND, is the windiest city in the world.

ADÉLIE LAND, ANTARCTICA, is the windiest place on Earth. Wind there blows almost constantly and its speed can reach 169 knots (195 mph).

EHÉCATL— Aztec god of the wind

OLGA FADEEVA is a children's author and illustrator based in St. Petersburg, Russia. Her illustrations for *Wind* were shortlisted for exhibitions in Italy and China, and they were also honored with an award at Moscow's International Illustration and Book Design Competition—Image of the Book. *Wind* has been translated into Chinese, German, Italian, Serbian, and Turkish, and it is Olga's English-language debut.

LENA TRAER is a freelance Russian- and English-language translator with a focus on books for children and young adults. She has also translated a variety of scientific materials for Russian-speaking audiences, including medical journal articles and subtitles for the *Science Today* video series by the California Academy of Sciences. Lena lives in San Francisco.

First published in the United States in 2023
by Eerdmans Books for Young Readers,
an imprint of Wm. B. Eerdmans Publishing Co.
Grand Rapids, Michigan

www.eerdmans.com/youngreaders

Text and illustrations © 2020 Olga Fadeeva

Originally published in Russia as *Bemep* by Rech

English-language translation © 2023 Lena Traer
English translation rights arranged through Syllabes Agency, France

Manufactured in Canada

31 30 29 28 27 26 25 24 23   1 2 3 4 5 6 7 8 9

ISBN 978-0-8028-5599-2

A catalog record of this book is available from the Library of Congress.

Illustrations created with acrylic, collage, and digital media.

The author would like to express her sincere
gratitude to Ludmila Kiseleva, lead engineer at the
Meteorological Information Department at the Arctic and
Antarctic Research Institute, for all her help.

Eerdmans Books for Young Readers would also
like to thank Jill Holz (B.S. Geology and Geophysics, M.Ed.,
and National Geographic Certified Educator) for sharing
her scientific expertise for the English-language
edition of this book.